PRINTHOUSE BOOKS PRESENTS

Boobie Boy

Miami's Urban Chronicles; Volume II

Thomas Barr Jr.

True Fiction

Thomas Barr, Jr.

©Thomas Barr Jr.; 2017

PrintHouse Books, Atlanta, GA.

Published: 5-15-2017

www.PrintHouseBooks.com

VIP INK Publishing Group; Incorporated

All rights reserved. No parts of this book may be reproduced in any way, shape, or form or by any means without permission in writing from the publisher, or the author, except by a reviewer.

Boobie Boy

Cover art designed by SK7.

Editor: Shelby Oates

ISBN: 978-0-9978116-81

Library of Congress Cataloging-in-Publication Data

#2017937577

1. Urban Literature 2. True Fiction
2. Religion 4.Thomas Barr Jr. 5.Miami, Florida

Printed in the United States of America

Thomas Barr, Jr.

In writing this novel I drew from past experiences and tales of the street. This novel is dedicated to the Rhoulhac family, my kindergarten teacher Ms. Gaskins, my parents, Alesha, Timothy, Latoya, Chewanda, Crystal, the Barr family, the Fulmore family, the McGee family, the Brown family, the Witherspoon family, Dr. Jake Miller, Dr. Richard Milner IV, The City of Miami Gardens, in the spirit of Carol City Cartel, E-Fro, Kenneth Williams, The click and the City of Miami.

Boobie Boy

Boobie Boys : Miami's Urban Chronicles Volume II, an urban literary fiction which portrays a biopic of career criminals in the drug trade set in the international city of Miami.

Neighborhood friends are enticed by the lore of money and power to sell drugs. The trials and tribulations faced by minorities are comparably different from their nonminority counterparts. For the main character "Kaz" his desire for money and power leads to his detriment as a leader among his childhood friends.

Kaz raised a moral man of standards with southern roots by his parents; has followed all the societal norms of the traditional education and career track realization of the American Dream. He is sucked in by the South Beach lifestyle and engages in Cocaine cowboy style shootouts throughout the city. As he navigates the climate of the Miami night life which can't be taught in school he confronts the dignity of truth.

Thomas Barr, Jr.

PRINTHOUSE BOOKS PRESENTS

Boobie Boy

Miami's Urban Chronicles; Volume II

VIP INK Publishing Group, Inc.

Thomas Barr Jr.

Atlanta, GA.

Boobie Boy

www.PrintHouseBooks.com

Thomas Barr, Jr.

Table of Contents

Chapter 1:	The Meet pg 9
Chapter 2:	Palm to Expressway pg 19
Chapter 3:	Miami Strip Club 14 pg 26
Chapter 4:	Murder pg 33
Chapter 5:	John Lee Murder pg 40
Chapter 6:	Lou Dowis pg 47
Chapter 7:	Shooter pg 54
Chapter 8:	Colors Apartment Complex pg 60
Chapter 9:	The Cantrelle Murder pg 69
Chapter 10:	Car Chase pg 76
Chapter 11:	Armed pg 83
Chapter 12:	Silver Lakes pg 90
Chapter 13:	The Drug pg 97
Chapter 14:	The Hold pg 104
Chapter 15:	Prison pg 111

Boobie Boy

Chapter 1
The Meet

The bars rang out as a man in a prison cell raked a makeshift dinner utensil back and forth along its surface. The inmate spent hours honing a razor sharp edge on the plain metal spoon. He obtained it from his service duty in the chow hall. He basically was letting his cell block mates know he had a shank and could protect himself.

In prison life the players know a key asset to keeping opponents at bay was that of unpredictability. Being deliberately unpredictable will throw the enemy off balance and keep them hesitant in regards to confrontation. Most inmates are remanded to operating in the most animalistic of social interactions. The adept inmates know what it takes to navigate this type of environment.

"Cut that fucking noise out man!" Said Kaz.
"Fuck that! I need to let these clowns know who they dealing with," said the inmate.
"People know who you are in here slick, I

know you, you're from Carol City right?" Kaz inquired.

"Why, you a fucking cop?" The inmate replied. Kaz shrugged off the slight.

Kaz had long ago realized that reputation was the cornerstone of power. Appearances are the gauge of judgments. Your reputation gives you a degree of control on how you're judged. It distracts from knowing the real. Kaz knew the value of the reputation of his hood and would use it accordingly,

"Man I'm from Lake Lacem projects," replied Kaz.

"Oh, you home team," said the inmate. "You heard of Beebee?"

"Nigga everybody know you!" Kaz shouted.

"Yeah, well why the hell you in here?" Inquired Beebee.

"Same as you negro—dope," said Kaz.

"Man you don't know nothing about no dope," said Beebee.

He stopped making the irritating noise with his utensil and focused his attention on Kaz in the neighboring cell.

"I know you run with a crew known as the

Boobie Boy

Boobie Boys and they run the Carol City section of Miami in the dope game," said Kaz.

Beebee eyed Kaz with suspicion. He was cautious to entertain the inquiries of his new cell block mate. He had heard of informant Miami detectives placed in cells to draw out word on the street from big mouth suspects. Beebee knew he would really have to vet this guy to see what he was actually about.

"So you with the Heard Boys," stated Beebee.

Kaz lay on his bunk as he contemplated Beebee's words. The Heard Boys were brothers who hung around with their friends at a local candy store in Carol City. Kaz knew they ran a small time operation selling weed to locals. They were also known as territorial about their neighborhood and who they associated with in the community.

"Naw man, I run solo," remarked Kaz.

"Well, if you ran with my homies you probably could get some real work," said Beebe. Kaz was curious now; he sat up on his bunk and spoke candidly. He was unsure how serious Beebee was. He could see directly where the conversation was going and the intentions behind what was being spoken.

"What you mean by that? I'm eating man! I get money," said Kaz.

"I tell you what, you're home team. I'll bring you into the Boobie Boy camp, we can get money and be the biggest game in Miami," said Beebee.

Kaz knew culturally Miami was divided and each community had its own mode of operations. The Latin community consisted of largely Cubans, Dominicans, Nicaraguans and Hondurans as well as the White neighborhoods. The Northwest of Miami was largely African American blacks, Jamaicans, Haitians and other Caribbean communities. Afro-Cubans, Afro Nicaraguans, Afro-Hondurans and other Afro-Latinos operated in isolated societies within the Latin neighborhoods. Kaz reasoned a dedicated crew of mobilized hustlers could exploit the foreign ties to outside countries and prosper financially making millions.

"I've been reading some books from the prison library on **La Cosa Nostra**," said Kaz.

"You read?" Beebee asked.

Boobie Boy

"Yeah negro, I'm not ignorant," replied Kaz. "The organized way they carried out their business model is ideal for us," he continued.

"Fuck them spaghetti eating motherfuckers, you think they smarter than black folks," Beebee replied.

"It's not about that. We gotta have a blueprint of operations if we want this thing of ours to really work," said Kaz.

"You know you're an interesting nigga," said Beebe. "Ordinary black folks don't really read books like that. Hell, I've never even bought a book."

"I would advise you to never tell anyone that," replied Kaz with a terse laugh.

"The key to many secrets can be found in a book, my man," said Kaz. "These people ran their organization working together and made lots of money."

Beebee fell silent for a moment; no sound was heard from his cell. Kaz could tell the wheels in his head were turning. He was being given an alternative view of how he was operating in the streets and he knew he needed change.

Thomas Barr, Jr.

"The thing is to have rules or commandments for movement in these streets, man," said Kaz. "Number one, no snitching and Number two, always know the movement of your crew. Maintain transparency with all personnel," he added.

"Yeah," agreed Beebee. "The ten *cocaine* commandments," remarked Beebee with a chuckle.

Kaz entered the recreational yard of the prison and met up with Pablo his old partner from the neighborhood. Pablo had been with Kaz from the beginning and was the muscle when they got in tight predicaments. Kaz sometimes referred to Pablo as "Blow", he came from a Latin background and was nice with his hands. He once won a street fight by knocking a grown man out. He was tall with a solidly built frame and was quick on his feet when evading trouble in the hood.

"What up Blow," he said.

The two gave each other dap as they leaned against a nearby wall and scoped out the recreation yard. The yard was largely concrete and was segregated

Boobie Boy

by race with the Blacks, Whites and Hispanics in opposing corners. There were neutral spots for weight training, basketball and fitness training. The day was sunny and the yard was busy with men milling around talking and shooting the breeze.

"Man I'm so sick of this place, I'm glad I only got a week left," said Pablo.

He stood against the wall and dangled a cigarette between his fingers. He raised it occasionally taking quick puffs before blowing smoke circles. Cigarettes were as good as money on the yard and could buy a person many prison 'luxuries'.

"Yeah you're lucky," said Kaz. "Let me get a Newport?"
"We're both lucky; you'll be out in like a month—that's no time."

The two men continued to lean against the wall, talking while taking in the view they had over the yard. Kaz could feel the smoke bellow through his lungs as he pulled from the cigarette and paused for a minute before exhaling.

Thomas Barr, Jr.

"This shit seems like weed," said Kaz.

"Damn my nigga you that clean?" Replied Pablo.

"Man we haven't smoked *shit* in 36 months, Negro," stated Kaz.

"Don't worry, we'll be back in business before you know it," said Pablo.

"You're so right," replied Kaz. "I linked up with Beebee."

"Boobie Boy Beebee," replied Pablo.

"Yeah, we're going to make some major moves on the outside, cuz," said Kaz.

"Fuck yeah!" Pablo responded.

"Doing this time got me doing a lot of thinking and I want to make real money. Not just money for fresh gear and a ride. I'm talking worldwide travel, yachts and big houses. Like '*They* live on Fisher and Star Island?' kinda gossip," said Kaz.

Star Island rested in the inter-coastal waterway of South Miami Beach and downtown Miami. Million dollar mansions lined the neighborhood and all the backyards of the estates contained docks attached to thousand dollar yachts. Kaz remembered how he would go there with his mother and how the kids his age would Jet Ski with their friends. He often wished he could've joined them; they lived a different reality and his view of life was vastly different in comparison to theirs. His mother worked long hours as a maid in those big houses and Kaz was inspired at a young age on acquiring wealth so he wouldn't have to do something like that.

Kaz formulated his own crew for the purpose of achieving that life and recruited Pablo as his right hand man. Hustling in the streets of Miami had its ups and downs. Unfortunately, prison and death were the negative components of the lifestyle he chose to pursue. Kaz had come to realize that the lifestyle was an addictive one and people loved a guy who was talented. It could be basketball or football, but whoever displayed a talent was exalted above all others. Kaz himself was not good in sports and he was uninterested in school. College was not in his plans. He thought of himself as exceptional in the streets though, scheming up ways to get money was his motivating factor.

"There go Beebee over by the weight benches," said Pablo.

Thomas Barr, Jr.

Kaz leaned off the wall taking a step forward and squinted towards the direction Pablo had indicated. Beebee was working on the bench press with a few of his boys. They were joking around and talking loudly as other inmates milled around watching them. Beebee had a knack for putting on a show. He was of a medium build but was cut with well-built muscles. He was known to challenge bigger guys fearlessly if he felt crossed. He was also known for shooting people with no hesitation. He seemed to have no conscience and if it came down to brandishing a gun to prove a point he was the wrong person to fuck with.

"Let's go, time for your introduction," he said to Pablo as he flicked his cigarette to the ground.

Chapter 2

Palm to Expressway

Kaz took a pull from a twisted joint he slipped from his back pocket. He stood on a desolate street in Miami as he puffed. The smoke from the joint bellowed out of his nose and the corners of his closed mouth. A few cars drove by with individuals waving to him and bidding him a good afternoon. He'd been out of lock up for about a month and was looking to turn a profit in the rough streets of Carol City. He'd gotten word that Carlo and Shawn ran a crew out of his old hood during his time inside. Carlo and Shawn were slangin' chronic to the fiends at discounted rates and had a loyal customer base. Pablo approached Kaz as he enjoyed the last of his smoke.

"Carlo and Shawn rolling real good, they got the whole block on lock," said Pablo. Kaz took another toke and coughed as he let the smoke go from his lungs. He then looked at Pablo and smirked. He had learned while in the streets it's a dog-eat-dog world. The only thing that mattered was survival. Yeah he could have negotiated a deal so that everyone could share in the profits. But why? Why stall out when the obvious thing is sooner or later someone was going to get greedy and attempt a takeover. It was best not to waste time and to just get to the crux of the matter he reasoned.

"Yeah negro, we'll see what they do when they have to close up shop," replied Kaz.

"You spoke with Beebee yet?" inquired Pablo.

"Not yet," answered Kaz.

"Word is he got out last week," said Pablo.

"He knows where to find me," replied Kaz.

"He's probably knee deep in some pussy," joked Pablo.

Kaz knew prison could break a man's spirit. Homosexual activity runs rampant when a man is without a woman for years. In a lot of cases the toughest guys get poked or poke others in order to relieve the sensation of being with a woman. Some guys are completely turned and by the time they come home they're straight up undercover brothers. This often results in a drain on the community resulting in the spread of aids and other detrimental factors upon former inmates. So, one could be sure that Beebee was not falling into those statistics; he most likely was doing exactly what Pablo said.

"That's good to hear as compared with the other motherfuckers from cell block four," said Kaz.

"Yeah," responded Pablo with a laugh.

"Once we line up with Beebee we will need to take over the block street by street," said Kaz.

Carol City was a middle class residential sector for Blacks and Latinos. The surrounding neighborhoods were mostly lower middle class and project home areas. Most of youth congregated in the projects and near the surrounding parks. Carlo and Shawn were known to operate near the parks of the projects.

"We would probably need to flush them out onto the streets or catch them on a highway or something," replied Pablo.

"Good thinking Blow, we need to avoid any school zone charges if we get caught" said Kaz.

Thomas Barr, Jr.

A black impala sat in a side alley off the street; it likely belonged to a local shop owner in the neighborhood. It had tinted windows and no readily identifiable characteristics that made it stand out. Pablo hotwired the car and the two men jumped in and exited the scene.

Kaz instructed Pablo to stop off at a nearby stash house and the two men armed themselves with two AK-47 assault rifles to do so. These were the choice weapons of the streets and when they were put to work they struck the most fear out of all other fire arms. People scattered-when they heard the staccato sound ring out. Kaz loved the sound the weapon made and often commented that it was like music to his hears upon squeezing the trigger.

The two men drove the stolen car to the area where Carlo and Shawn were known to hang out. They parked in the cut and waited for the two to make an appearance; it was late afternoon and almost dusk. The sun was going down and the nightlife was just starting to pick up in the neighborhood. They soon spotted Carlo walking from the park to a house on the comer of the block. Shawn pulled up to the house in a box, light blue Chevy with all white

Boobie Boy

interior which he parked on the street. A group of young men gathered around as Shawn's car radio thumped with the base enough to shatter windows. Kaz cocked his AK-47 insuring the rifle was locked and loaded. It had been awhile since he fired the gun and it felt heavy in his hands. Pablo sat in the driver's seat serving as the backup gun. He mainly would drive the car and track the marks to insure the hit was a bulls-eye mark.

Carlo soon jumped in Shawn's car along with two other guys and the car pulled off heading out of the neighborhood. Pablo screeched off in pursuit of Shawn's car. With the loud music blasting Shawn was unaware they were being followed. The cars roared down 27th Avenue towards the Palmetto Expressway. Carlo's vogue tires hugged the road and seemed to glide the vehicle along like a sail boat. Kaz gripped the rifle in anticipation of the hit and made sure the safety was clicked off. He could feel his heart race as the engine revved on the Impala. Glancing at his partner's face he could see that he was tensed. Shawn's car pulled through a yellow light and maneuvered onto Palmetto. Pablo went through the light as it turned red and accelerated alongside Shawn to make the hit.

Kaz got his footing and leaned out of the passenger side window with the rifle. He could see all the faces in the car go blank with fear as he squeezed off the shots.

Rat-a-tat, tat, tat. The AK sang out as cars on the highway hit their brakes and the smell of burning rubber filled the air. The hot shells of the gun bounced inside of the Impala burning Pablo as he swerved the vehicle to the left. Kaz sprayed the side of the light blue Chevy with bullets before being slung in the back seat. Shawn's car veered off the road and hit the side rail as nearby cars screeched to a halt on the roadway. Pablo regained control of the car and punched the gas accelerating to the nearest exit.

Kaz looked out the back window of the speeding car at the chaotic scene he and his cohort had just caused. Cars were at a standstill as smoke covered the roadway from the burnt rubber of eighteen wheeler trucks and automobiles. Pablo took the exit off into a residential neighborhood and slowed his speed to avoid suspicion. They drove to one of the deepest known canals and sank the car along with the weapons. Kaz knew the canals of Miami were the best place to get rid of hot stolen vehicles. The waterways were so deep that it would be months before anything was found in them. Many times the police with their frog men were hard pressed to find discarded stolen vehicles in the deep canals anyway.

The first step of taking control in Miami had been accomplished by Kaz and he was now ready to meet with Beebee to implement the rest of his plan. He knew eventually that he would have to deal with the repercussions of the Palmetto hit. He would just temporarily co-op some of Shawn and Carlo's crew and slowly take over their customers. In allying with Beebee, the Lucern Crew would be enhanced by more street level soldiers, stronger firepower and more distribution markets in the hood. The loose affiliation would seek to make everyone involved more money and with more money comes more power.

CHAPTER 3
Miami Strip Club 14

Kaz parked his dark green Chevy in the parking lot of the Rolex strip club and sat admiring the scene with his windows down. The Rolex was a lively spot where all the ballers and sexy females hung out. The strip club traditionally is a place for men to spend their hard earned money. This club was more of a social club where both male and females gathered for fun. Kaz lit a Black & Mild cigar as he scoped out the scene and frowned as he inhaled the pungent tobacco smoke. He let out a huge cough as the smoke poured out of his lungs onto the dashboard of the Chevy. As he continued his smoke he noticed the girls arriving in their late model BMWs and Mercedes Benz whips. He thought to himself in amusement just how much the girls made in a night.

"Give me the keys to the Chevy nigga, this a jack move," he heard someone say.

Boobie Boy

Kaz sat as stiff as a statue and did not move. The cigar remained clutched in his mouth at a tilt and the smoke was really starting to burn its way down his throat. He could feel cold metal on the back of his neck and dared not to look around. The voice broke down into laughter and the cold sensation dissipated.

"Damn, nigga I was just playing. You were scared as hell," said the voice.

Kaz dropped his head and knew instantly who his assailant was. He should've known from the start that it was Beebee but could not figure out the disguised voice. It threw him off because it sounded like a Bahamian accent. A lot of the street cats from Miami played around with disguising their voices with accents. They used this facade to commit robberies and other type of criminal acts. Miami was so multi-cultural you couldn't help but be influenced by the diverse cultural practices.

"What's up nigga, what you doing out here?" Beebee inquired.

Kaz watched as Beebee turned his back to the building of the Rolex; shielding himself from the view of passers-by. Beebee slipped a chrome-plated .40 caliber into the waistline of his belt and lowered his shirt over it. Beebee was known to pack a pistol and now that he was out of the joint he stayed strapped.

"Trying to be like you, looking for something to fuck," replied Kaz still puffing on his cigar.

Kaz slid his arm across the interior leather seat of the Chevy and popped the door latch unlocking the door.

"Get in negro," he said to Beebee.

Beebee walked around the car and opened the passenger door. He adjusted his gat along his waistline before sitting and closing the door. He reached in his back pocket and pulled out a clear pint sized bottle of cognac. He took a long gulp before nestling into the leather seats of the Chevy. Kaz imagined Beebee felt good sitting in a nice clean box Chevy with a candy apple paint job. Kaz had previously dressed the car up with Trues and Vogues rims upon his return to the neighborhood. He got a lot of compliments on the car and at one point considered putting it in the local car show.

"I heard you did some house cleaning my nigga," said Beebee.

"Yeah, I still put in work when need be," replied Kaz.

Beebee offered Kaz the bottle of cognac and he took it. Before Kaz took a swig of the alcohol he removed his cigar and gave it to Beebee. Kaz knocked back a shot of the cognac and then knocked back another. Beebee watched him for a moment before taking a drag of the burning cigar.

There was an unspoken code among cohorts and partners. This code was one of brotherhood and being down for your homie. The code was what allowed you to pass the bottle or the smokes to your home team without hesitation. A bond that spoke volumes in the hood and acted as an unspoken truce.

"Well it's on my nigga, I got my mans and them at the Port, dem Columbian niggas are going to send them chickens through any day now," said

Beebee.

The words slipped from his mouth with so much ease and he spoke in a convincing manner as to assure Kaz it was no big deal. He seemed a real pro at this game and his reputation preceded him. The streets were well aware of what Beebee could do and now that he was back home he was a more determined man ever.

"With your weed connect and those ganja smoking customers of yours we could blow up in this town," said Beebee.

Kaz dealt with the Zoe Pound Boys, most Haitians were real true hustlers. They raced speed boats along the coast and made drops. They were good at getting bales of weed through to the intercostal waterway networks of the south. Beebee knew of Kaz's affiliations but had no idea of the vast networks he was about to be privy to.

"Well, I heard you was on pussy lock down; I hope you've tied up your loose ends," said Kaz.
"I'm gonna tell you a little known story—me and the homies around the way would hold bets.

Boobie Boy

We would bet five g's for the person who dated a girl with the nicest set of boobs. The boobs had to be perfect and for all purposes flawless. No stretch marks, no blemishes, of equal size, no fat, all boob," said Beebee.

Kaz could tell the cigar and the cognac were getting to Beebee. As he spoke he began to accentuate his words when he tried to make a point. He started to use his hands to describe what he was talking about. His head bobbed back against the seat as he visually imagined his description of the perfect set of tits.

"This bet went on and on. The pot grew from $5,000 to ten grand, my nigga," said Beebee.

Kaz could see how such a thing could happen. You have a lot of dope boys who don't really know a lot about having money. They do a lot of spending on material things and do little investing. A lot of ego spending goes down which usually takes place in strip clubs, on race cars and on huge gambling bets. The ones who do wise up build rap empires, real estate business and catering restaurants.

"Who finally won the bet?" Kaz inquired.

Thomas Barr, Jr.

Beebee was staring out of the windshield and caught sight of something. He squinted and wiped his eyes.

"Oh Shit, there go that fuck nigga, be right back," he said.

Beebee jumped from the car with a quick stride and walked up to a convertible red Camaro with its top down. Kaz's hands gripped the steering wheel as he watched the exchange between Beebee and the seated man. Beebee pulled his .40 caliber to shoot but nothing happened. He then tried to cock the slide barrel back, but it was too late. The man in the Camaro pulled his gun and fired point blank at Beebee. Beebee fell back from the car holding his ripped shirt as the bullet had glazed his shoulder. Kaz hit the gas on the Chevy screeching to the exit of the strip club parking lot. Beebee jumped in the opened door as Kaz peeled off burning rubber down the street.

"You one wild Negro," commented Kaz.

CHAPTER 4
Murder

Andy Stranton was a local tough guy from the Baha projects of a Carol City neighborhood. He tooled around in a low-rider pickup truck with low profile tires and dark tinted windows. He was a well-known hustler in the hood and was a thorn in the side for Beebee when it came down to the dope business. Andy grew up in the hood and was not a friend of the group Beebee ran with. However he was well known in the neighborhood and his parents ran the local comer store.

Andy's mother emigrated from Saudi Arabia. In pursuit of the American dream, she acquired a stable business to support her family. Andy dabbled here and there in the dope game but was not viewed as a threat by other peddlers. Pablo didn't like him though and thought he was a greedy bastard.

"What's up Blow," said Andy.

Andy stood on the sidewalk by the store as Pablo entered. Andy's customers usually found him at the store when they were looking to score a hit. Many in the neighborhood patronized the store because it was conveniently located and sold anything a customer could imagine. If there was a need for loose cigarettes, they sold 'em. If you needed to purchase a single stamp instead of a book, you could. The store accommodated the patrons' needs and that's what made it popular.

"What up Andy, you good?" Replied Pablo.

Pablo entered the store as Kaz remained outside to smoke his Black and Mild.

"Get me a brew negro," he yelled to Pablo.

Kaz lit his Black and began to take short puffs from it. He often did this in order to get the tobacco to burn faster making the fire catch readily. As he smoked he eyed Andy making hand-to-hand sales. There was a crew of guys over by Andy's truck shooting dice as onlookers watched the action.

"What up K, you want a piece of this?"

Boobie Boy

Andy asked.

"I'm good man," replied Kaz.

Kaz didn't care much for gambling, he was no good at it which probably is why he didn't care for it; dice were very popular in the hood and many played regularly blowing thousands of dollars in less than ten minutes. The thing about dice is you have to pay attention, be assertive and know the game to avoid getting cheated. Dice were fast-paced and all the players had input on interpreting the rules.

Pablo came out of the store with two beers and passed one to Kaz. He had bought a scratch off lottery ticket and was attempting to scribble the card with a quarter he got as change from his purchase.

"Forget that scratch off, Blow you need to get in this game," said Andy.

"Man, I'll take all you fools' money," replied Pablo.

Kaz was familiar with one major vice his partner obsessed over and that was gambling. Pablo was a compulsive gambler. He won big because he played big, but when he lost it was devastating.

Andy snatched up the dice interrupting the current game and shook them in his hand.

"Let's go baby, money on the table," said Andy.

Andy's crew was all hustlers and hundred dollar bills seemed to appear with the snap of a finger. Kaz knew Pablo was exceptional with the dice and had watched Pablo win big on some of his rolls.

"Let me get tens, my nigga," said Pablo.

He took the dice from Andy and rattled the two ivory squares within the palms of his hands.

"I'm gonna roll a four for you niggas," exclaimed Pablo.

Pablo let the dice fly from his hand and they skirted over the cement hitting the back wall of the store. One die rolled a three and the other rolled a one resulting in the total of four rolled on the shot. Pablo scooped the dice again and rattled them for his next roll.

Boobie Boy

"You niggas better get your money up!" He yelled:

Kaz knew if Pablo rolled a seven or eleven he would crap out. He also knew Pablo was fond of calling off his number which angered players on occasion. The rule is you can call off by saying *Not pass*, which basically means you're betting that you can't roll the same number again. In addition you can't roll a seven or eleven while the dice are in play on the bet site.

"Yes," yelled Pablo.

The dice rolled a five and he scooped up five one hundred dollar bills. Kaz knew he would continue until he quit or crapped out. It also depended who had the deepest pockets to be able to end the session and walk away with the winnings. Often times cats got sour about losing so much money in such a short span. Andy and his crew naively bet against Pablo's call so they lost money. They continued to bet against Pablo's calls and Kaz was now feeling uneasy as the situation tensed.

Kaz knew the danger in playing dice games. It's

hazardous if you are not playing with friends or people you're not cool with. The game is very flexible and even side bets can be placed on the main game that is being played. Andy's crew had no love for Pablo as he continued to roll and snatch up the thousands off the cement sidewalk. Kaz noticed a flash out of the corner of his eyes and soon heard a shot. One of the crew had offered up gunplay so Pablo quickly stabbed him in his arm. The group broke in reaction to the exchanges with all the players sprinting in separate directions.

In all the mayhem, no one realized that Andy lay bleeding on the cement sidewalk. His body twitched as blood gushed from his lower abdomen. He apparently had been shot when his homeboy pulled a chrome plated pistol only to be stabbed by Pablo.

Kaz imagined the entire incident would bring heat on the block. He and Pablo fled the scene but returned later to scope out what was occurring in the aftermath. Paramedics escorted by cops were all over the place and Channel 7 News trucks soon arrived on scene.

"Any witnesses?" Inquired a news reporter.

Boobie Boy

"We're still in the middle of questioning," answered MDPD Sergeant Alex Casado.

Kaz recognized the officer from the many Channel 7 News reports he appeared on at crime scenes. He was a burly man with a Cuban background and had been on the Miami Dade County force for years. He spoke with an accent and maintained a slick combed back hair style popular for the times. Sergeant Casado was also a veteran on the streets and he was the typical law man with a sense for justice.

The crew of investigators canvassed the area attempting to turn up witnesses to the crime. They roped off the store entrance with yellow tape and blocked off the street obstructing the flow of traffic through the neighborhood.

"Now we can take Andy's corner," remarked Pablo.

Kaz contemplated Pablo's words as they watched the scene displayed in front of them. He had not imagined Andy's fate would come to this, but this incident would prove beneficial for the advancement of his plans for the block.

Chapter 5
John Lee Murder

Kaz met Beebee and Charles Lee at Under the Tree eatery. It was a local hang out spot in Carol City and everybody who was anybody hung there. The place served American style burgers with fresh hot chicken wings. Conch salad and pork sauce were also delicacies prepared by the cooks of the joint so the menu was diverse and slammin'. People milled around outside the place meeting friends and discussing neighborhood rumors. Girls came out in their Sunday best and the guys were dressed to the nines pushing freshly waxed vehicles.

"I see a lot of violence swirls around you and your boys," said Beebee.

"Look who's talking," countered Kaz.

Charles Lee was a close associate of Beebee's and Kaz was familiar with him from the neighborhood. He went to school with his sister Stella and she was one of the finest girls in class. Kaz remembered many a day when Charles would come up on school grounds and beat on chumps trying to talk to his sister. The group of men now stood outside of the hangout near the doorway entrance.

"By the way what happened to the money from the crap game?" Inquired Beebee.

"My man Blow had that covered, he's always 'bout that loot," said Kaz.

"Well, like I said before, we all about to get that loot," replied Beebee.

Two cars drove along the streets with booming stereo systems. One car was a candy apple red Chevy with dark tints and the other car was all black with low profile tires. The windows in the building rattled as the cars made their way up the street. People greeted Beebee as they passed and entered the restaurant.

"We're going to meet up at Momma Love's spot later and chop it up for a bit," said Beebee.

Momma Love lived in a duplex off 183rd Street near a county water treatment plant. She had a daughter who was friends with Beebee. Her house was a split level duplex with a huge two-car garage. She was the neighborhood candy lady and kept all kind of snacks in her cupboards for sale to the kids.

Charles Lee and Beebee were already at the house when Kaz arrived with Pablo late that afternoon. They all gathered in the garage which was somewhat converted into a dayroom with a couch. A beige table sat in the middle of the floor and a color TV sat in the corner of the room near the closed garage door.

"Welcome gents we have a package arriving and we need to come up with a plan to move this weight," said Beebee.

Kaz realized Charles was strapped with a .357 pistol and he knew Pablo was packing or at least had a blade on him. Kaz had no idea that this meet was going to be the start of buying weight and establishing business objectives. Beebee seemed to have a clear direction on how he wanted things to work and Kaz knew his own connections were very much needed.

"We got a shipment coming in off the port

Boobie Boy

and we need to break it down for distribution," said Beebee.

Beebee's soldiers were located at strategic places throughout the neighborhood and all business was done by word of mouth. They hustled from their location where they were stationed on an hourly and daily basis. There was no going to clubs or any other place trying to push drugs on people. Instead the customers came to the product and if no one knew you or vouched for your buy, then no deal.

Beebee's connection originated out of the country and poor promotional job opportunities for black dock workers made it easy for recruitment. The Longshoreman was the key in overseeing successful shipment for flooding the market.

A white work van arrived at the house with a driver and two passengers. The van was parked inside the garage. The Brown twins, Tim and Rocky unloaded the packages into stacks on the table. The Brown twins were Boobie Boy associates and were killers on pay roll. They were well armed and ready for action at all times. A man dressed in an all-white linen suit soon appeared on the scene and was bestowed with many nods of acknowledgement. Kaz wondered who the stranger was who had arrived with the shipment and upon listening closer to the chatter among Beebee's soldiers he found out it was Blandon the supplier and connect for the Boobie Boy Crew. Rumor had it that Blandon was a Nicaraguan business man, but it was obvious his business was in the drug game.

"We got fronted fifty keys and we need to turn the profit on them within a thirty day time frame," said Beebee.

Fifty keys was a lot of dope and Kaz knew that this was no easy feat. In his experience in the game he knew connects were very serious about keeping time lines. He thought Beebee had placed them in a bad position in hooking up this deal. He didn't feel good at all about their predicament.

"That's where you come into play homeboy, we're gonna need you to give up your network to help us move this weight," said Beebee.
Kaz soon felt hesitant about giving up the details of his distribution network and was under the impression his partnership with Beebee would be

mutually independent. He did not count on the mixing of the two to further the interest of one organization. Kaz felt that this could be the formula for later trouble, but right at the moment the weight had to be moved. It was a rare thing to get fronted so much dope and if it could be flipped the money would be in the millions.

"What's the worth of using my network?" Asked Kaz.

"Fifty keys nets us a $750,000 cut, my nigga," answered Beebee, "and a hundred keys is a minimum profit of $1.5 million on the street," he said.

Kaz knew Beebee was accurate with his numbers. In weed sales profits were much lower with a diminished chance of doing real prison time. He had seen many of his counter parts make $15,000 a key selling to sub suppliers. Profits could also be made in the ballpark of more than tripling the money by breaking it down with cut or baking powder.

Kaz's network consisted often of dope houses scattered throughout the neighborhood. Different spots garnered a different customer level and this was reflected in what was paid on a buy. There were the twenty dollar sales, the hundred dollar sales, the one thousand dollar sales and the five thousand dollar sales. The houses were not run down like the crack dens in the city but were actually nice. They were protected with heavy entrance way iron doors and were flush with TV's.

Beebee's networks were more street level with dope spots littered throughout the neighborhood. He had about seven spots he called honey pots because of the money he made regularly from them. He devised a plan to utilize one of the houses in Kaz's network as a count house for the money. Another house would be used as a cook house to cook crack cocaine and breakdown the product. As a partner with Beebee all proceeds would be on a 50/50 split and workers would be paid in respect to their duties. Beebee was always movin' to spread the wealth with the community. He even held yearly cook outs in the park and sponsored youth fund raising events for the locals. The plan for ingratiating the organization into the community was an ingenious one, but jealousy always rears its ugly head.

CHAPTER 6
Lou Dowis

Kaz and Beebee sat hunkered over a table processing work at one of the dope houses in the hood. Small baggies and glass vials were generally used to hold the processed drug for distribution to customers. Kaz often wondered how so many baggies and vials could be purchased without raising the suspicions of the public. He learned from one of the other dealers that small amounts at a time could be purchased at smoke shops without concern and that smoke shops often had detailed logos on the baggies making them more attractive to customers. Larger order amounts are often obtained from a manufacturer. These companies generally sell the baggies to medical supply companies, the pharmaceutical industry, retailers that sell small screws and fishing lore companies.

"Everybody feeds off the dope game," commented Kaz to Beebee.

"Yeah, and I'm at the front of the line,"

replied Beebee.

Pablo charged into the kitchen almost knocking over the table where Beebee and Kaz were working.

"Damn nigga, you almost knocked this shit over!" Exclaimed Beebee.

"Yo, two niggas from the Heard Boys clique robbed our pushers and kicked them out the hole," said Pablo.

"What happened, Blow?" Kaz inquired.

"Word is the dudes drive a white drop top Camaro and they've been beefing that the hole was theirs," replied Pablo.

"Man, go find them niggas," said Beebee.

Kaz knew instantly that this was a major issue and it would not end with positive consequences. He and Pablo hit the streets while Beebee remained at the spot wrapping up the work.

They looked for a suitable car in the hood that was unlocked and hotwired it in search of the identified soon-to-be victims. Hotwiring cars in the hood was as essential a skill as covering one's tracks

Boobie Boy

while committing acts of deceit in public. Kaz had picked up this trick in prison by talking with career criminals and car theft specialists. Most expensive and modern cars hid the wiring with a fancy, designed interior display. So most of the older common cars are often the ones selected by robbers for stealing.

Kaz used a flathead screwdriver to break the hidden locking pins in the car they targeted and then unscrewed the plastic covering from the steering column. The key is identifying the correct wiring connector in all the jumble of wires. Kaz identified the three main bundles and pulled out the wires leading to the battery, ignition and starter steering column. The battery wires are always red, the ignition wires brown and the starter wire yellow. Kaz cut the ignition and battery wires twisting them together. He then took the starter wire and skillfully sparked it with the battery wire. He finished by using the flathead to break the steering column as Pablo hopped in the back seat.

The two men drove around the hood for a couple of hours looking for the white Camaro to no avail.

"Negro we've been out here two hours, where

are they?" Inquired Kaz.

"They're right there nigga, put the car in park," replied Pablo.

The two men put on their masks and bullet proof vests. Kaz cocked his Glock nine and placed it on his lap. Pablo dressed in all camouflage, cocked an AK-47 and made it ready to fire. The white Camaro sat at a gas station across the street and two men exited the vehicle unaware they were being watched. Pablo hopped from the back seat and began firing his weapon at the two. The men sprinted away from the car and tried to find refuge as bullets bounded around them.

Pablo jumped from the car and bore down on the AK with every bit of power he could muster. Kaz heard Pablo's weapon jam as the bullets left the nozzle of the gun, but Pablo just cleared it with the quickness and cocked it again, slamming even more ammunition in it for further assault. People screamed as they tried to dodge the spray and one of the men fell hard from an abdomen shot.

Pablo then chased the other around the side of the store to a fence and shot him in the chest.

Boobie Boy

"It burnsss! …hurts…so much," said the man.

Pablo pumped another bullet into the man and the victim slumped onto the fence in a bloody heap. Kaz was still at the driver's door of the car; he gave a whistle as he had lost sight of Pablo. Pablo stepped towards the slumped body and placed the barrel against the head of the man. He pulled the hairline trigger of the AK47 and with little effort blew the base of the man's skull apart bloodying the fence.

Kaz jumped into the vehicle as he saw Pablo running back towards the car with the AK down by his side. They had just shot down two men in broad daylight and essentially started a war. Kaz slammed the gear shift of the car into drive and the car screeched out onto the roadway out of sight.

They now had to get rid of the getaway car and any evidence that could link them back to the incident. Kaz drove to a predestinated spot in the warehouse district and wiped the car clean of any prints. Pablo took a piece of cloth and stuck it in the gas tank. He took a lighter and lit the rag. They then tossed the ski masks into the car along with the guns and departed the scene. The car flamed up as they dipped out and the tank blew up engulfing the entire vehicle in flames.

Kaz parted ways with Pablo and crashed at one of the safe houses in the neighborhood owned by his network. He felt uneasy about the death of the men, especially the one Pablo murdered. He did not support black-on-black crime. He had difficulty rationalizing it as just a cost of doing business in the hood. In all the cities in the nation black-on-black crime had been an issue in regards to hazards in the community. Kaz could not help feeling dismay, but he reasoned if he could give back more to youth community groups it would be ok.

The killings at the gas station freed up any controversy in regards to the disputed dope hole in question though. In general a common spot in the city generated a profit of $3,000 a day. The hole operated 24 hours a day with pushers taking shifts every eight to twelve hours depending on rank and sale activity. If the spot is pumping and money is flowing no one leaves for fear of losing money. The people that make the most money generally get promoted and gain more responsibility.

In the streets there are a number of ways to survive

and make money. A person can progress quickly by way of moving up through the ranks of the dope game. An individual can also rob and steal their way up the ranks. And like Pablo, a soldier can develop the skills of a relentless killer and become an enforcer faster than most realize.

The enforcers are the fear and control that managed the masses in an organization. If they are in turn controlled well by the boss players then individual kingdoms can be established. Kaz and Beebee were the boss players that were building an organization to rival that of the Cocaine Cowboys of South Beach and Miami Beach.

Kaz sat alone sipping on a double shot of Hennessy XO. He felt a rumble in his stomach. He kicked his chair back from the table and ran to the toilet. He vomited as soon as he got there, dispersing all the liquor he had just drank. He hated the site of blood and tissue matter and it seemed that even if he could convince his mind to push the gas station scene out of his thoughts so he could focus on the bigger picture—his gut wasn't going to let him forget.

CHAPTER 7

Shooter

Hollywood and Fats were associated with the Heard Boys. They owned a car wash off of Hill Avenue. And, once the two in the white Camaro were killed, the gas station murders spread through the hood like wildfire and speculation mounted on who was behind the killings—especially at the car wash. Kaz regularly patronized the wash as the guys there were the best in servicing candy paint vehicles. His dark green Chevy sported a candy polished paint job that required work keeping a shine on it. Kaz took it there as a ritual when he had to get it washed. The guys at the wash would reprimand Kaz for washing his car with regular soap powder. . They always insisted it damaged the paint removing wax and sealants which protected the car from the South Florida elements so he became one of their regulars so they could treat his paint job right.

The car wash was also a good place to find out what was going on in the hood. Much like the barber shops and the hair salons of Miami it was a place for gossip. People would come and talk about anything that was affecting their lives. From crime to politics, who was fucking who and even who was smoking that rock. It was a news pipe line and if you were new to the community the car wash was the place to learn the neighborhood.

"You want a wax on this today Kaz," inquired the wash attendant.

"Naw man, just a wash," replied Kaz.

Kaz was not as high profile as Beebee. He was able to navigate the hood with less attention. Kaz knew before he met Beebee that he had a standing feud with the Heard Boys and this would make it hard on business. However fear was an effective motivating factor and this tool proved useful in garnering a rep on the streets.

Kaz sat in a nearby wooden chair and watched the attendant rinse down the Chevy with an industrial water hose. The water flushed over the top of the car trickling down the sides onto the windows. He soaped up the rag and began washing the exterior of the car in a circular motion. Other cars were being washed in the lot and Kaz made note of the fact that the place was always crowded. He did not see Hollywood or Fats in the vicinity but had a notion they were around.

People milled around the wash waiting on their vehicles. Kaz overheard snap shots of conversations as he sat patiently. People discussed many topics including the gas station murders. He did not realize that so many witnesses saw the deed and were commenting about it publicly. As he sat still watching the attendant with his vehicle, Hollywood walked out of the office and greeted him.

    "What up, K," said Hollywood.
    "What up man," replied Kaz.
    "I see work being put in," said Hollywood.
    "Man go 'head with that; I'm about peace my nigga," said Kaz.
    "Listen man, I don't have no beef with you, but your boy and them matchbox niggas need to ease up. It's a lot of money out here and everybody can eat," said Hollywood.
    "Yeah, I hear you, 'Wood," said Kaz.

Kaz listened intently as Hollywood was trying to make his point. In the streets one must know how to read between the lines. Hollywood was basically trying to relay a message to Beebee and reason with Kaz about his stand on how things should be.

"Hey Jack, don't charge this man—he good," said Hollywood to the attendant. The attendant washed the car down and dried it off with the sham.

Kaz took Hollywood's gesture as a token of peace. Kaz knew how difficult Beebee could be when it came to these type of situations. It didn't help things that Beebee didn't personally like Hollywood and he made it well known.

Kaz sat outside Briscoe Park in his freshly washed Chevy. The park was a local hangout in Carol City. People in the Carol City community had regular picnics and other festivities there. DJ groups would set up walls of speakers, turn tables and microphones. Some groups would set up grills and cook while the bass from the speakers beat like exploding bombs. The players in the neighborhood would drive by or profile in their cars like a car show. Some guys would loosen the bolts in their trunks and it would rattle when the base dropped in the music.

Kaz liked to flirt with the girls in the park. As they

walked by admiring his ride he tried to hold conversations with them. He liked it when they would put on their best gear and sashay through. They would wear their hair pinned with the short bob cut. In addition they wore gold bangles and big Latifah earrings. Kaz loved to gaze at the phat booty of a pretty woman in tight jeans. Kaz also enjoyed the music the DJs played in the park.

There were a number of DJ groups in Miami that competed to be the best. The Miami rap music sound consisted of fast paced beats and heavy base. DJ groups would just set up at a moment's notice and bump music for horns in the hood. The best groups in the hood were Triple M DJs, Ghetto Style DJs, Jam Poney Express, Space Funk DJs, DJ Nice & Nasty and the Bass Master DJs.

Kaz noticed Pablo in the park socializing with some of the neighborhood regulars. He still felt uneasy about the gas station incident and decided not to approach him. He thought he should keep some distance between them until things settled down. Pulling the trigger of a gun is easy but living with that action can be hell. The face and essence of the person tends to linger with you always.

Boobie Boy

It takes an ice cold persona and an "I don't give a fuck" conscience to live through such a traumatic act thought Kaz.

Pablo it seems had these characters in abundance and his conscience was obviously clear about the incident.

Thomas Barr, Jr.
Chapter 8

Colors Apartment Complex

Kaz was unseen by Pablo and he fell back camouflaged by the crowd. He proceeded back to the Chevy and accidentally bumped into a woman.

"Excuse me," she said.

Kaz could see that she was very good looking. From first contact the aroma of her perfume lingered in his nostrils. She had designer gear and the tight jeans he was fond of seeing on attractive women.

"I'm sorry, I'm Kaz," he said.
"Nice to meet you Kaz, I'm Tanisha," she replied.

Kaz was smitten by Tanisha's good looks and pleasant demeanor. The conversation flowed smoothly between them and he got her number. He had not been very successful with the women he dated. He seemed unable to develop a deep relationship which often led to superficial attachments. Upon going to prison and again on release his focus was entirely concentrated on making substantial amounts of money.

Tanisha was the polar opposite of the females Kaz associated with. She was a strip club bar owner in the city. She was intelligent and confident which Kaz detected from their conversation. He knew instantly that he wanted her and he could feel the vibe of interest from this woman towards him. He decided he would pursue her and see what developed. However, he mentally questioned himself about the feasibility of being in a relationship. His lifestyle was one that called for sometimes staying up all night. Leaving for meetings at a moment's notice and addressing unforeseen problems at any hour of the day. His life was basically unstable and it would be unfair to impose that on anyone. He also wondered how he could tell anyone that he was a drug dealer. He owned no other business and could not explain how his money was made.

Kaz was now running the organization in conjunction with Beebee from the home base on 183rd Street. Momma Love's duplex proved to be the best cover because it was a duplex. The boys worked out of the back of the unit bagging up packages. The neighborhood was active so it proved to be the perfect cover to hide in plain sight. Kaz's distribution network proved efficient in processing orders for keys and Beebee's network expanded out of state with his associates on regular rotation to visit the duplex to arrange pickups.

Then there was Charles who was becoming more dissatisfied with his dope spot over at The Colors Apartment Complex. He was breaking down ounces and selling them from ten to twenty-five dollars a pop in rock or powder form. Kaz suspected he was buying them off Beebee for about 1,800 dollars an ounce. He was more than doubling his profit margin on most of his sales at the spot. Kaz suspected Charles was becoming greedy with the increased work they were getting from the supplier.

Momma Love ran the duplex with all the skill of a Wal-Mart manager. She kept the place clean and organized. It was far from a hangout spot and no one loitered outside the unit at any time. Any traffic for dope sales was diverted to the dope holes and safe houses in the surrounding areas. A lot of the ride-by traffic was the local pimps and players of the city. They rode up in Cadillacs, Mercedes Benzes and Jaguars. They traveled with an entourage of body guards and women in short skirts. Then you had the rock customers who were desperate for a hit and were loyal returning customers.

"Man that fuck nigga, Bolly is always taking my customers," complained Charles.
"You mean that nigga over at the 'plex," said Beebee.
"Yeah, we got into it the other day about that shit," commented Charles.
"We may need to go see that cat," said Beebee.

Kaz could sense a major problem brewing and he knew Beebee was ready to take action on behalf of Charles. Kaz felt guilty about not kicking it with Pablo lately and thought it would be good to pull him in on this.
"Listen Beebee, why not let the soldiers handle this," said Kaz.

Kaz was aware of the teachings he learned from his elders and the OGs in the hood. He imparted this often on Beebee whenever he got the chance.

"Let others do the work for you. Never do yourself what others can do for you, Negro," commented Kaz.

Beebee pondered for a moment before responding.

Kaz could see his wheels turning and gave him the time to consider the words spoken. Such assistance saves valuable time and energy. Such a move also gives the aura of efficiency and speed which could be used to strengthen leadership.

"Ok cool. ...so are you gonna do it?" Beebee questioned.

"Hell no, I'll get my boy Blow to handle it," responded Kaz.

The Colors Apartment Complex was the project tenements built like condo style housing units. People were always milling around outside. It was one of the major dope spots in the city and a lively spot for robberies. Bolly usually sat on an outside stoop of one of the apartments selling dope and shooting the breeze with his cronies. Pablo and Charles set up just down the street from Bolly on beach cruiser bikes rented from the beach. They pulled on their ski masks

Boobie Boy

and swung out two AK47 choppers and rode by the stoop firing. Bullets bounced off the concrete building as Bolly and his crew dove for cover. People started running as the pair continued emptying their clips in attempt to hit their target.

As the shooters cleared the scene Kaz and Beebee sat parked across the street in a low rider truck with dark tinted windows. They surveyed the area and determined pretty quickly that Bolly was dead. Sirens and medical emergency trucks were heard in the distance. The low rider truck silently rolled down the street and around the comer escaping the disorder.

The count house was located in North Miami not too far from Joe Robbie Stadium and it was full of girls counting money. As the deals were made and the money flowed in the count girls certified the correct amounts. Money often arrived in duffle bags or boxes from dealers, suppliers and associates. The count house was a buzz about the drive-by that went down at The Colors Apartments. News reports indicated two people were dead to include Bolly and a three-year-old killed from a shot to the head. Kaz knew Charles and Pablo would have to lay low for the next couple of days to divert suspicion. Beebee made it clear to them to remain tight-lipped about the incident. A child had been killed and the public was outraged blaming the police for lack of control. A total of 88 bullet casings were gathered from the scene and the police made the block *hot* interviewing witnesses.

The hood generally had a no snitching policy among the neighborhoods. Many viewed the movement as criminal attempts to persuade informants not to cooperate with law enforcement. Officials denounced the campaign stating it was more to frighten the people with the information from reporting activities to police who were often viewed as the enemy. The youth of the community, specifically black males heralded the slogan.

Kaz realized this hit and the community it fell in was a dangerous mix in the hood which could affect business. In shaking things up and waking up the sleeping masses in the community, attention was now being directed to the streets more than ever. The streets were his domain and they were how he ate; so Kaz was determined to eat at all costs and this meant operating in a more discreet manner.

Kaz and Beebee remained in the count house until

everyone had departed. They split the profits and allotted a kickback to invest in the business. They would make all the payoffs and reup the supplier for the upcoming month.

Kaz knew that Beebee was interested in expanding the business nationally. Kaz was unsure of the next move though as they had solicited too much attention locking down the block.

Kaz had remembered the sayings of an old OG, an Original Gangsta from the neighborhood and he was wise in the quirkiest of ways. Kaz would often rush by him on the street while headed to school in his early years.

Hurrying denotes a lack of control, always seem patient as if you know things will go your way eventually, the man would say.

"What are you gonna do about this expansion idea of yours?" Asked Kaz.

"I told you man, we can double or triple our profits if we do this," replied Beebee.

"I don't know man, I think we got too much

heat on us," said Kaz.

"Man in *this* business we're always going to have heat. You gotta take a chance," said Beebee.

Beebee had a point. In business one had to be willing to take risks or leaps of faith to get ahead of the crowd. It is also true that one must be ready to lie in one's own bed and deal with all resulting consequences. They had made the determination that they were going to take over the city—and so it had begun.

CHAPTER 9
The Cantrelle Murder

Kaz sat on a bar stool at Secrets, a strip club and bar in the city. The patrons were mostly older, working class men. Some dyke women as well as heterosexual females frequented the club on occasion as well. Tanisha was the major owner with the backing of some female friends, all whom were strippers back in the day. After years of saving they put up the funds to buy the place and made Tanisha the manager. Tanisha had worked her way through college and raised her kid while dancing. She luckily had the foresight to plan her future and save her money when the times were good.

"You should've told me you were coming, I would've set up a table for you," said Tanisha.

"I'm good, I wanted to surprise you," replied Kaz.

He liked when she pampered him and catered to his desires. It made him feel normal as if he were an "Ordinary Joe". Although she was a confident person,

Tanisha knew how to treat people and make them feel special. As a manager she had developed these key customer service skills in her work.

"I like the place, you seem to be doing quite well," stated Kaz.

"Yeah, we've definitely put work in the place," replied Tanisha.

Women walked around topless with bikini bottoms. Some wore nothing at all and those were the ones that got bigger tips. Kaz noticed the one gold pole located behind the bar and imagined girls acrobatically scaling it for large tips to pay the rent.

"Did you ever imagine that you would own a club like this?" He inquired.

"I had no choice but to dream and plan, I had a kid to raise," replied Tanisha.

In that split instance, Kaz wondered about the choices individuals make on life's journey. He reflected about his position and wondered if it could have been different. *Could he have made a different decision and made a different living for himself?*

Boobie Boy

The bar began to fill up with customers and the bartender prepared ice buckets of beer for the happy hour crowd. The DJ played fast paced booty music and the women shook their money makers. The older guys began showering the floor with money as the young girls took off their bikini bottoms. Kaz marveled at the power these women had over the crowd in that particular instance. He imagined what Tanisha was like in her days as a dancer.

"Are you staying for happy hour, I can set you up," said Tanisha.

"Naw, I got business. I'll catch up with you later," replied Kaz.

The brief dose of the bar's atmosphere was enough to clear Kaz's head. He had some decisions to make and plans to develop. He left the bar determined to get a handle on his festering problems.

Kaz arrived at Carol Mart, a neighborhood flea market commodity shop. He usually got his hair cut there by Buddha. As he was walking in the door he heard his name called. It was Hollywood sitting in a sky blue Nova with an all-white interior.

"What up K, let me holla at you a minute," said Hollywood.

"What's happening man," replied Kaz as he approached the car.

"Have you had the chance to speak to your man?" Inquired Hollywood.

"Naw, I haven't seen him. He's been keeping a low profile lately," said Kaz.

Kaz stood at the passenger side window as they spoke. The interior of the car was extremely clean. The whiteness of the leather seats made the inside of the car seem blindingly bright. Kaz noticed the butt of a gun sticking from under the seat where Hollywood sat. There was a closed pint of cognac on the seat next to Hollywood.

"You're a smart guy K, you can run the streets without that dude," stated Hollywood.

"You got cats that'll unite under your flag, cuz," he said.

Kaz knew what Hollywood was saying was true. He had linked up with Beebee for the purpose of making big money. His distribution network had more than served as an asset for their business successes. Other

Boobie Boy

people could see that he was more than an asset to their movement and that Beebee was just a hot head.

Kaz knew in order to survive in this jungle he had to be formless. By having a visible plan one opens oneself up to attack. Instead of taking form or being visible to your enemy keep yourself adaptable and on the move. Kaz postulated the best protection is to be as fluid as water.

"I'm a simple man, I don't need that attention," replied Kaz.

"Man, fuck that! Get money, nigga," said Hollywood.

Kaz knew Hollywood and his crew made a lot of money in their dope spots. However he was doing well in his endeavor with the Boobie Boys. Hollywood's comments were haunting and could generate a lot of shake up in the hood. If such an action was implemented it would effectively monopolize dope sales. The smaller rival dealers would have no choice but to merge with such a massive organization. The main problem in that plan would be the disposal or the complete elimination of the current top reigning dope lords.

Thomas Barr, Jr.

As Kaz entered the flea market he pondered Hollywood's proposal of allegiance to him in controlling the dope flow in Carol City. It was an enticing offer and the money would definitely be a good thing. However Kaz knew Hollywood could not be trusted. This thing was chess and not checkers. Hollywood would have a lot to gain in such a move for himself. He would be trading off one problem for a lesser problem so to speak. He hated Beebee and for him Kaz seemed a lesser threat to him.

Kaz was careful to control his tongue in his encounter with Hollywood. He monitored his reactions to what Hollywood was proposing. He thought it prudent to tailor his behavior in response to Hollywood's inducements. Kaz knew in this business being unabashedly open leads to being predictable and familiar which makes it almost impossible to be respected or feared. If a person is neither respected nor feared then they will not have power.

While in prison Kaz had crafted certain skills which allowed for his survival. Training himself in concealing his intentions was one of them. In mastering such skills it allows for the upper hand in dealing with people under certain circumstances. Kaz believed that this certain circumstance was a pivotal one which could determine his evolution in the dope game. He would use Hollywood as a means to an end.

Kaz entered the barber shop and Buddha motioned for him to have a seat in an open chair. The shop was crowded with patrons but Buddha knew the days Kaz came in for his haircuts. Buddha had an extensive clientele base and kept an ear on the streets. He knew a lot about what was going on in the hood. He prepped Kaz for his cut as other barbers feverishly worked in the busy shop.

"Same cut boss," inquired Buddha.
"Yeah Buddha, tighten me up man," answered Kaz.

Chapter 10
Car Chase

Kaz met up with Beebee at the count house in the city. It was a night after a big sale and they usually sat for hours divvying up the cuts. The count house was more like a hangout spot and party house. People who were not in the business and were essentially squares were clueless. Only the people in the know were actually aware of what the place really was. Beebee had paid about 250,000 dollars for the purchase of the house and had renovated the place.

Beebee's setup consisted of mostly girls doing the actual count. They were in turn overlooked by security and the count was finalized by a boss. Beebee determined what cuts were done and who got what. The sales were now averaging 100 kilos a week and this averaged about 3 million dollars a week.

A cat named Blandon had become a regular fixture around the Boobie Boy crew and tonight's party was no different with him in attendance. Rumors ran rampant of his activities and associations. He was

Boobie Boy

said to be closely tied with the governing family in Nicaragua. His wife was said to be some big food contractor with that government's National Guard. He was believed to be from one of the largest land owning families in the country. Kaz viewed him as an enigma of a person. He was hard to read and he masked his intentions very well.

Beebee had girls all over the city and any car he wanted he bought it cash money regardless of the price. Every day was a party in the Boobie Boy camp and the money flowed freely. For anyone that was affiliated with the Boobie Boys they essentially had a free ride and paid for nothing at the parties.

Blandon and Beebee worked closely together in closing deals. Whatever Beebee could move Blandon would supply. Beebee eyed expansion into the immediate southern states of Georgia and Alabama. Kaz knew this move would be major and would bring more scrutiny from challengers to include the alphabet boys of law.

. "So what's my cut?" Asked Kaz.

"Same as always, nigga, half of my cut," replied Beebee.

Thomas Barr, Jr.

"Here, take a bonus," said Beebee. He threw a key of cocaine on the table. It was still packaged and was pure with no cut. Kaz knew he could get $15,000 easily off it in a straight sale to a street level dealer. If he really wanted to turn a profit he could cut it with baking soda and quadruple the money; he could easily net about $60,000 or more off a key and with that kind of money be set for the future for sure.

Blandon was also very generous in the giving of gifts and money with associates of the Boobie Boys. He gave the count girls diamond bezel bracelets sometimes when sweet deals were completed. He also sponsored parties and other neighborhood activities in efforts to earn respect from the crew. Blandon supplied bowls of cocaine at his parties and attendees were treated to catered delicacies of gourmet food.

Kaz knew Blandon was more powerful than he let on to be. There was always speculation on what ties he possessed in the drug trade. His ability to generate keys for purchase was almost limitless. Beebee marveled at how much work Blandon was able to bring from outside the United States. Beebee made

Boobie Boy

sure Blandon was good in the neighborhood and no one fucked with him. Blandon, on the surface was very basic and he wore no bling whatsoever. The only time he was flashy was when he wore suits while out clubbing with the guys. Kaz respected Blandon but had his reservations about him.

When the count was done the crew would get drunk and hit the strip clubs for late night partying. Kaz looked forward to this time and used it to bond with the crew.

Kaz sat behind the steering wheel of a Delta '88. Beebee sat on the passenger side of the vehicle and loaded a 12 gauge pump. The car was stolen from the parking lot of a shopping center and was in use to track Fats. Fats was Hollywood's second in command in the dope hustle. Beebee had gotten word that Fats was selling on his turf and wanted to catch him red handed. Kaz thought it was foolish of Fats to cross Beebee in such a way. It was well known that Hollywood and Beebee had issues. Fats arrived in the projects near the park. He stood on a stoop alone smoking a cigarette and hustling to the trickle of traffic that carne thru.

Thomas Barr, Jr.

"This motherfucker is on my block trying to clock," said Beebee.

"Man you sure about this," inquired Kaz.

"Hell yeah, nigga," replied Beebee.

Kaz hit the gas on the idling Delta and the old car jumped into gear screeching down the street. Fats was on alert upon hearing the revving car and jumped into his Buick Regal. He skirted off down a side street and around a comer. Beebee hung out the window and fired a few rounds in the back of the Regal. Fats lost control of the car and skid head long into a light pole. Kaz pulled the Delta alongside the crumpled car and Beebee got out to inspect the damage.

Beebee walked up to the vehicle and fired two blasts from the pump inside the car. He ran back to the Delta and the two men fled the scene.

As they drove in silence hovered inside the car, only the engine of the old Delta was heard. Kaz knew in taking out Hollywood's second in command a war was about to erupt in the hood. It seemed more gang related activities were arising among factions. The money making aspect of the hustle venture was being overlooked. Kaz did not like the path they were on and was unsure of what could be done to change it.

They ditched the stolen car before arriving at the count house on foot. It was night time and the darkness helped conceal them. Blandon met them out front in a black four door sedan. He had two .22s concealed in the trunk of his car with a silencer and a silver plated Uzi.

"Give me the Uzi," stated Beebee.
"I got this stuff from some of my associates; I knew you boys were putting in a lot of work in these streets," said Blandon.
"I'll take this .22 along with the silencer," said Kaz.
"Kaz my man, I got this just for you," said Blandon.

Blandon opened the back door of the sedan and pulled a grenade launcher from under the seat. Kaz and Beebee looked at one another in amazement. They both had dropped jaws and were surprised at what they saw.

"Damn man this is what they have in the military," said Kaz.

Kaz knew with this kind of firepower they could not be stopped on the streets. He also reasoned the police presence in the hood would increase due to the violence. Business may suffer if cops started busting perspective buyers. He knew Beebee was all for violence and would not be deterred from this harmful direction. Kaz would have to let things play out as they were and hopefully a resolution would present itself.

"Whatever you guys need I can get it," said Blandon.

"Cool we're going to need more of these guns," replied Beebee.

"The next shipment will be here soon," said Blandon.

"We'll be ready and waiting," responded Beebee.

Boobie Boy
CHAPTER 11

Armed

Kaz initially met Tanisha at Secrets near the bar area during her work hours for a drink. She soon had him set up in VIP with a bottle of Gray Goose. He sat at his table and sipped on his cranberry vodka with a sliver of mint leaf. He pondered on how he has been under pressure with conscience heavy from all the killings that were occurring.

"Do you want something to eat," inquired Tanisha.

"Naw, I'm not hungry," replied Kaz.

"Well, you need to eat. I'll order you up some wings," said Tanisha.

She bounded off towards the kitchen and stopped momentarily to wipe down tabletops as she went. She was always moving about and never stationary as she carried out her duties as a manager. *She seemed so happy and content in her professional position in life*, thought Kaz to himself. While making his way in the street and getting money he felt as if something was missing. He didn't feel stable and having a "peace of mind" is an essential part of existing in a comfortable space for oneself.

Tanisha returned with the order of chicken wings and sat down next to Kaz at the table. She watched him as he downed his drink and poured up another for himself. Kaz sucked down the refill and prepared another shot.

"You need to eat or you're going to get wasted," she said.

"Let me ask you, what would you do if you could retire right now with millions?" Said Kaz.

Tanisha paused for a moment. She tapped her fingers on the tabletop and seemed puzzled by the question.

"I don't know, I love what I do now," she answered. "What would you do?" She inquired.

"I would move to the Bahamas and go into the chicken farm business," said Kaz.

"The chicken farm business," said Tanisha with a frown.

"Yeah, that's productive and simple living," replied Kaz.

"I can see living in the Bahamas but as a

Boobie Boy

chicken farmer? I don't think so," said Tanisha. Kaz took one of the wings in between his fingers and twirled it around; he took a bite and grimaced from the vinegary taste of the hot sauce.

"We have been westernized to chasing the dollar and living complex lives," commented Kaz. "Success does not require having a lot of money, it's the belief about yourself and making the commitment to take control of your life that matter," said Kaz.

Tanisha looked in his face in amazement. She was surprised that he was revealing himself to her in this way.

"Is the real Kaz trying to come out in there," she said pointing to his head.

Kaz smiled broadly as Tanisha arose from the table to attend to awaiting customers. He continued to munch on the chicken wings in his plate. He wondered if he had scared off Tanisha with his vivid dreams of being a chicken farmer. He wondered if that was too small a goal in comparison to her aspirations.

"Puck it!" He said loudly to himself.

The music was now blasting in the bar and people began to file into the VIP sitting area. Usually all the self-proclaimed ballers had reservations in this area of the club. Bottles of alcohol ranged in the hundreds of dollars. Many street level hustlers came to this spot to flaunt their money.

As he sat at his spot he noticed a familiar face in the crowd. It was Pablo and he eventually made eye contact with Kaz as he proceeded through the crowd. He approached the table alone and sat down. He took a wing from Kaz's plate and bit into it like a ferociously hungry pit bull.

"Damn negro, you want a drink?" Offered Kaz.

Kaz poured him up a vodka and cranberry juice. He finished off the chicken and flicked the bone to the floor. He grabbed the drink and guzzled it down; he wiped his mouth and slapped the glass down on the table.

"You've been MIA, what's up?" He inquired.
"Putting in work, same as you, bruh," replied Kaz.

Boobie Boy

"It's hot out there for me, man. Instead of making money on the block, I'm out there ducking cops," said Pablo.

"You're the one that agreed to be Beebee's personal hit man," replied Kaz. "That's slow money."

"Something else has gotta work for me, man, this shit is bugged out," said Pablo.

Kaz could see the Pablo was reaching. He wanted to know if Kaz would shoot him some work or money or something. Kaz realized that this was an opportunity to get at Hollywood with a plan.

"Listen I got some things on the burner and you could partner up with me if you're down," said Kaz.

"You know I'm your man K, anything is better than the shit I'm in now," said Pablo.

"Ok Blow, I'm gonna hook you up. Just be on standby," said Kaz.

Kaz arrived at Momma Love's duplex on 183rd Court Street and saw Charles Lee outside smoking a cigar. Charles Lee was always around whenever a shipment came in or work was available for distribution by the street level hustlers. Kaz found it suspicious because he would always question where the supplier's transport originated.

"What up Lee, you seen Beebee?" Asked Kaz.

"Nawman," answered Charles.

He seemed edgy about something. Kaz's antennas went up and he decided to nudge Charles more.

"You cool man, you acting like the Police," said Kaz.

"Nigga I ain't no PoPo," he shot back in an agitated voice.

"Cool out, I'm just fucking with you man," replied Kaz.

"Yo it's dangerous to play like that," said Charles.

"Yeah, well tell your man I'm looking for him," said Kaz.

Kaz left Charles to his smokes and entered the duplex. Momma Love as usual was sweeping the floor and doing other busy work. Four guys sat around a table playing cards and taking bets. Many of the hustlers enjoyed betting among the crew in

Boobie Boy

order to display their wealth. The thought nothing of losing thousands of dollars among their comrades—it gave them a twisted sort of bragging right. The games went on for hours and many took part in doing side bets on the main game.

"What up with Charles?" Asked Kaz.

"Shit I don't know, something's always up with that nigga," replied Momma Love.

She continued about her cleaning not looking up.

He sat down and watched the game.

CHAPTER 12

Silver Lakes

Kaz sat in the back seat of a brown Lincoln Town car with Pablo at his side. Beebee and Charles sat up front with Beebee at the steering wheel. Beebee liked to hold court in which he talked about business strategies. Charles sat hunched over rolling a blunt between his fingers. When he lit it the heavy aroma of the weed permeated the interior of the Lincoln. Beebee had the windows rolled up tight and the A/C was blowing cold air. They sat parked as the blunt was being passed.

"Pass me that shit," said Beebee.

"My nigga this is that dope shit," said Charles.

"K, I was meaning to commend you on your people," said Beebee, "That network of theirs is making big money."

"Making money ain't no problem with them," said Kaz.

"Well we branching out of state to the Carolinas, Virginia and Maryland," said Beebee.

"Cool I'll hit the road with no problem," said

Boobie Boy

Pablo.

"Yeah, I just got a load of scanners from Blandon—that nigga is up on his game," said Beebee.

"You do know you got to learn the codes the cops use," replied Charles.

"That nigga gave us all that shit," responded Beebee.

"How'd he know that?" Asked Kaz.

"That nigga knows everything, took him about ten minutes to explain to me," said Beebee.

"That nigga was supposed to get me a Mack 10 but he never showed up," said Charles.

"I heard he got pinched by the Peds," said Pablo.

"Yeah, well I don't know about that," replied Beebee.

"You know I've been having a personal problem with that nigga Big Bo," said Beebee.

"Big Bo from the Silver Blue Lakes apartments?" Inquired Kaz.
"Yeah I heard that nigga was talking about robbing you and shit," said Charles.

Kaz's eyes were getting watery. The smoke from the blunt was beginning to bum his eyes causing irritation. Beebee started the engine and pulled the car into traffic towards the apartment complex. The blunt was in full rotation as the men anticipated what would happen on their arrival. As the car pulled into the complex Beebee spotted Bo standing on the curb near the parking lot. Beebee lowered his window and pulled a chrome-plated .9mm from under the seat. He fired one shot and hit the gas on the Lincoln. Kaz looked out of the back window as the car sped off and saw Bo sprawled out on the ground.

> "Man you hit that nigga," said Pablo.
> "Yeah he's laid out on the ground," said Kaz.
> "Let's get back to the spot," said Charles.

Beebee maneuvered the Lincoln through the neighborhood and resumed a normal speed to avoid detection. Kaz knew there were a lot of bystanders that witnessed the drive by and was anxious. Beebee had disregarded all precautions and reacted out of pure emotion. This action was indeed detrimental to operations. Beebee parked the car in the yard of one of the safe houses he owned and used a car cover to conceal it. Big Bo did not pose an immediate threat to the functions of the operation. He was a mere small time street hustler with probably a hundred dollar operation. Kaz wondered if there was something more to that situation and was resolved to keep an ear out for any relevant rumors. Kaz was also concerned about doing dirt around Charles, as he was suspicious of him. He was resolved to take more steps to insulate himself from him.

Beebee sat at the table playing a round of spades with the crew. Kaz sat on a nearby sofa and watched guys bet on the game. Mother Love was not home and the duplex was alive with music and people drinking beer. Blandon walked in the duplex with a couple of strippers. Kaz recognized them from the bar and hoped they would not recognize him. Tanisha must have given them the night off he thought to himself. Blandon was dressed in a white linen suit and all the girls wore tight jeans that complimented their figures. Their cleavage was exposed in white lace blouses and the guys all gawked at them.

"What's up Blandon, I thought you were locked up," said Beebee.

"Yeah they got me with a couple of ounces and tried to throw the book at me," stated Blandon.

"Damn what happened man?" Inquired Beebee.

"Partying with this female I forgot I had the shit in my car," said Blandon. "They tracked my accounts back ten years."

"You get ruly time?" Asked Beebee.

"Hell I only got 28 months of probation, I keep the best lawyers," commented Blandon with a laugh.

"Damn you lucky as fuck," stated Beebee.

Kaz sat quietly listening to the exchange between the two. Beebee seemed enthralled with his story. He found it intriguing that Blandon had been caught with so much evidence against him but he still got off with a slap on the wrist. Kaz suspected Blandon had high level contacts and those contacts probably were very powerful. Blandon spent no time in jail and he seemed unbothered by the entire incident.

Blandon's situation did not attract much scrutiny. Many did not want to rock the boat in regards to the incident. Millions of dollars were being made because of the inexpensive price of his keys. Beebee definitely didn't want to kill the goose that lay the golden eggs so he made jokes about the incident instead.

Boobie Boy

The game of spades continued on and the drinking lasted to midnight. The strippers began to perform and the guys' attention turned from gambling to the girls. People liked it when Blandon was around. He always knew what it took to make a party come to life; he also supplied dollar bills to select members of the crew to party with throughout the night.

Kaz didn't want to get too involved in the festivities. He however watched how the strippers seduced and controlled the crowd with their dances. They twerked their hips and performed exotic lap dances. Dollar bills were raining everywhere and the guys were drunk from hours of drinking and they were absolutely riotous. The strippers seemed controlled and professional. They knew what they were doing and maintained control weaving their magic. Kaz imagined exercising this type of control over the street level workers in the organization.

Blandon and Beebee promptly excused themselves from the activities. They stood in the hallway having an intense discussion. Everyone was distracted with the strippers and was unaware of the aggressive exchange. Blandon soon walked out and Beebee returned to watch the strippers entertain. Kaz didn't know what to make of the exchange and continued to study the girls. He assumed the argument was somehow related to money and it was common for the two to haggle over it. The strippers worked the room well and their money bands were filled with bills. Kaz pictured Tanisha in this type of atmosphere and wondered if she had nights similar to this one.

Boobie Boy
CHAPTER 13
The Drug

Kaz and Pablo sat parked across the lot from Hollywood's and Fats' car wash. Kaz had discussed Hollywood's offer with Pablo and they were going to confront Hollywood together. Hollywood was outside his business and spotted the dark green candy colored Chevy. He approached the car.

"What's up, K, I would know this car anywhere," said Hollywood.
"Yeah, get in man," said Kaz

Hollywood opened up the rear door and slid in onto the back seat. He shot Pablo a quick glance.

"What up Blow," he said.
"Hollywood," replied Pablo.

They drove around Carol City, the traffic was mild that afternoon. It was a bright and sunny day. People milled around the neighborhood. Hollywood sat anxiously in the backseat not knowing what to expect.

"So what's up fellas?" Inquired Hollywood.

"I gave your offer a thought, and here's how it's going down," said Kaz.

"I'll front you a key and depending on how you handle it, we can continue to do business," said Kaz.

Kaz knew Hollywood desired more product and the possibility of branching his hustle to the next level. Hollywood was getting about $3,000 an ounce and his guys were hustling $50 dollar packages of cocaine but only making maybe $25 dollar profits per share. His crew was hungry and it was well known that he treated his guys poorly. Kaz imagined one could exercise considerable control over a group who felt slighted by their leader. If that was the case with Hollywood's situation he would attempt a takeover by proposing an irresistible deal.

"Word, that's what I'm down with," said Hollywood.

"Yo man I hope you don't fuck this up," said Pablo.

Kaz left Hollywood with a key and would see how

Boobie Boy

he could handle the product on the streets. Kaz used Pablo to oversee the transactions and movements of Hollywood's crew. They purposely focused on crack cocaine distribution. A lot of Hollywood's guys worked out of the car wash and also around the parks of Carol City. The crack heads serviced by Hollywood's crew became viciously loyal to them. They bought vast amounts of drugs· and brought more customers.

Hollywood proved just as successful to them as his crack heads were to his business in moving the key very quickly with customers waiting to return, all motivating Kaz to bring him fully into the business venture.

Hollywood's crew set up industrial cauldrons in abandoned warehouse buildings. In those buildings they broke down cocaine and cut it with baking soda powder. Once the baking soda powder was melted down it was poured in with cocaine. The drugs were then poured into plastic trays and covered in ice until hard. Once solid they were broken into pieces, weighed and bagged. Hollywood's demand for keys grew and the movement grew with it—to about fifty keys a month.

Beebee began to hear rumblings on the streets about clashes with Hollywood's underlings. They were butting heads with some of the Boobie Boys in the day-to-day drug sales on the block. Kaz suspected this would be the case and prepared for it by distancing himself from any connection to Hollywood by way of Pablo.

Beebee got word that Pablo was running the Hollywood crew, but before he could confront him, Hollywood shot him in a drive-by. He did not kill him in the attempt though.

Kaz had little contact with Beebee after the shooting and Beebee was resigned to keeping a low profile in the hood. Blandon had once again disappeared and rumors were getting to Kaz concerning possible looming indictments by the PEDs. Local police were investigating the many shootings in the hood and talks of snitching was rampant.

Kaz heard from a reliable source about Blandon's movements. Blandon had been caught in a DEA bust. He became a government informant to keep from going to prison for the rest of his life.

Boobie Boy

Blandon's contact was a cartel boss in Nicaragua and through this network tons of keys were moved to Miami. The Nicaraguan boss was affiliated with the CIA that supported the rebels in that country. The CIA allowed the boss to operate with impunity in shipping cocaine to Miami. Blandon, who was caught by the DEA brokered a deal through his boss' CIA affiliations. He was an undercover affiliate and no one was aware except for a select few in the know.

Kaz realized Blandon's contact was a direct source and that was the reason Beebee got the drugs for cheap. In getting the drugs cheap they could sell a better quality product at reduced rates. In comparison to the average dope sale in Miami it was a domination of the market. There was no competition for this pure a product.

Kaz came to know the decimation of the neighborhood was due to outside sources. The government apparently had knowledge of illegal drugs being smuggled into the city. His organization unwittingly participated due to their greed and lust to live the American dream. Blandon dangled money and the good life to entrap Beebee. Kaz knew now that his freedom was in danger and his new revelation may be too late. He would need to reach Beebee before Blandon in order to devise an exit or mitigation plan.

Hollywood was now on alert and he knew he had hurt Beebee. He smelled blood in the water and was circling to kill. Kaz had to deal with this issue in a delicate manner; he would need to coordinate with Pablo to telegraph his plan. Pablo didn't seem concerned about the issue and he apparently enjoyed being the kingpin in his appointed position. He was in a lucrative station and was making big deals with Hollywood. Pablo relayed the fact that Beebee was facing a possible indictment. Kaz knew that they saw Beebee as being in a vulnerable state. He was physically hurt and facing the wrath of law enforcement. The Boobie Boys now were being squeezed off the Streets. The leadership was in peril and gunfights on the street were common with the hustlers on the block.

Kaz was now concerned with the intentions of Pablo. He was getting harder to control in regards to his handling of the Hollywood situation. Kaz realized eventually he would need to get out of the deal with

Boobie Boy

Hollywood and simply cut ties. Boobie was nowhere to be found and Kaz was running the crew on his own. The crew had a diminishing supply of drugs on the streets. Sales were drying up because the pipeline Blandon facilitated was now dead. Other dealers were suddenly aware of the opportunities to capitalize on the downward spiral of the Boobie Boys. This would certainly result in the increase in product prices in comparison to the past street rates. The product would also be of lesser quality. In the dope trade the perception of inexpensive acquisitions is the driving force. Crack heads make money selling desired products at substantially reduced rates. Kaz knew this from the many times he was offered the same kind of deals. The quality of product put on the street would definitely go unmatched in relation to other competing dealers.

CHAPTER 14

The Hold

Kaz considered leaving town, but he needed to tie up all his loose ends in Carol City before disappearing. He knew there was a task force out to squash all the drug dealings and murders in the neighborhood. It was rumored the task force assembled for the job was a dubious click of dirty cops. They carried around drugs and often planted them on unwitting suspects to bolster their arrest records. They also harassed people in the neighborhood and beat up any loiterers they found on the street.

He was low on cash and needed a major deal to get away clean from the gangster life he led. There was no need to consider Blandon as an option for setting a deal because he was a dead man walking. He was resigned to contacting Charles and establishing a dialogue to facilitate a buyer. Charles was essentially Beebee's right hand and knew many suppliers who could put the word out.

Boobie Boy

Kaz was desperate for a deal and he contacted Charles through a street level hustler named Rico. Rico was cool with Kaz and he was also a longtime associate of Charles' going back before the Boobie Boys' affiliation. The meeting was setup at Momma Love's place and would be essential for possibly getting to Beebee.

Momma Love was home performing her usual house cleaning tasks and the place was rather empty. It was strange to see the place so vacant; there was almost always some type of gambling going on. Charles sat at a table drinking cognac from a tall shot glass as Kaz entered the front door.

"Nigga, I thought you would be out of town by now," said Charles taking a shot.

"Naw, what's up with Beebee?" Replied Kaz.

"He layin' low, what you want with me?" Charles asked.

"I got a key that needs to be moved, can you set me up with somebody?" Asked Kaz.

"I can set you up," replied Charles.

"Same rates," said Kaz.

"Cool, meet me back here in an hour," said Charles.

Kaz left the duplex in business mode and he knew he needed to be prepared for the meeting. He hoped to make the money and disappear for a while until things calmed down in the city. He didn't want to leave without Tanisha, but he knew she was well established in the community. The likelihood of her picking up and relocating was dismal at best He would say his goodbyes and disappear.

Kaz retrieved the package from one of the cold houses and stashed it in the trunk of his Chevy. He returned to the duplex and was there before Charles. Momma Love was in the kitchen making dinner and the house smelled of brown stew chicken. Kaz had not eaten in hours but he had too much to accomplish to worry about that now.

Charles showed up with two other guys. Kaz had not seen these cats before and was apprehensive. The guys were well dressed in sports gear and wore gold medallions around their necks. They displayed serious expressions and were very observant of the surroundings of the duplex. Kaz was hoping to make an across the table sell for about $15,000. This was more than enough to help him skip town.

Boobie Boy

Kaz gave the package to Charles who in turn exchanged it for the money. The two men immediately grabbed Kaz.

"DEA, you're under arrest!" They shouted.

Kaz was slammed to the floor and fitted with plastic handcuffs. Momma Love was then handcuffed and escorted from the home. Kaz could not see Charles and wondered if he had gotten away with the package or the money.

While Kaz lay face down in the prone position, agents entered and searched the premises. Kaz was quite sure they wouldn't find anything. Momma Love kept the place spotless. She didn't tolerate a whole lot of drugs and other paraphernalia in her presence at the duplex. The two agents returned frustrated and they seemed sure more was related to the bust than just a key.

"Where's Beebee?" Inquired one man.

"Who's that?" answered Kaz.

He felt a kick to the right side of his rib cage. He grimaced from the pain of the agent's boot to his side.

Thomas Barr, Jr.

"We got ourselves a smart ass," he hissed. Both men grabbed Kaz by the arms and sat him up on a nearby chair.

"We know Beebee's been selling guns supplied by his partner Blandon," said one agent.

"1 don't know nothing," Kaz commented.

The sound of two-way radios could be heard echoing through the duplex. Kaz could barely make out what the cops were saying on the radio. He did pickup that Charles and Momma Love were in custody. They were being transferred to metro for processing and lock up. Kaz was curious as to why he hadn't been transferred like the others. The agents were consulting with each other and looking for any other relevant evidence in the duplex. Kaz gleamed from bits of radio transmissions and conversations that the Boobie Boys had monitored for weeks now. There was also an unnamed informant who gave inside information on the activity of the members. Such investigations usually allow for intelligence intercepts, wiretaps and the accumulation of telephone records databases. Kaz was unaware that they were under such scrutiny by law enforcement. Kaz wondered who could be the rat that snitched out the entire undertaking.

Kaz was transported to the Miami Dade County Detention Center in Homestead Florida and booked for possession. He was granted no bail and assigned a court date to complete his hearing. He had no contact with the outside and wondered what was happening with the Boobie Boys on the street. Kaz later found out through the jailhouse vine that Charles was the snitch for the government. He was on the DEA payroll and had been notifying agents of all supplier transport times.

Charles had been associated with Beebee for years and it was out of his character to snitch to the FEDs. It has been known he got jammed up some years back, but for him to rat on his crew was shocking. Charles was a main enforcer and knew a lot about the hierarchy on who did what. Whatever was gleaned from his cooperation would be solid evidence.

Kaz knew that he would be offered a deal to corroborate all that Charles had reported during his debriefing. He immediately requested a lawyer before talking to any law enforcement official about his charges. Whatever was on the table would be negotiated from his legal representative of the law.

Kaz remembered as a youth how his friends would be tricked into confessions by the cops. They often were ignorant of their rights in the legal system as it relates to jail. Some figured because they were from a poor family they weren't afforded representation. Kaz had money stashed away for this specific scenario and because he planned for the incident he was ready. Kaz knew thinking ahead in this business could be a lifesaver. One must consider sacrificing in the beginning to truly reap the rewards of deeds in the end. Kaz knew he would be back out in the streets as a result of his own smarts in no time.

CHAPTER 15

The Prison

Kaz was out on bail and his attorney was fighting the charges on the basis of law enforcement entrapment. Charles working on behalf of the DEA facilitated the purchase and was the culprit his lawyer proposed. Kaz knew the best lawyers were aware how the game was played and who to play it with. Having money definitely leveled the playing field and balanced the masked scales of justice.

Kaz was back on the streets in his Miami neighborhood in no time, just as he had predicted. Momma Love's spot was now hot. P:ractically shut down the operation; the hub was at a standstill. Street level dealers began feuding amongst each other on certain blocks. Kaz knew the clock was ticking on his dope career. His opportunities were limited and he had only done what he saw his cronies do in order to get ahead. It was a definite mistake of judgment and he lamented the decision on a daily basis. However, he was in the middle of the problem and had to work through it to survive. He desperately needed to get into contact with Beebee.

Kaz arrived at Tanisha's bar early the following morning and it was empty accept for a few employees. Tanisha had not come in yet and Kaz sat watching the news on a nearby television above the bar. He was amazed upon seeing a picture of Beebee being flashed on the T.V. screen. The caption read:

MAN WANTED FOR MURDER AND DRUG CZAR CRIMES.

"Hey turn that up," shouted Kaz to the bar tender.

The attendant fumbled for the bulky remote and pointed it in the direction of the tube. The sound of the reporter became louder as he read off a list of alleged charges against the suspect. Beebee had just made the "Wanted List" and this was a dreadful title to have when facing allegations for murder and mayhem.

Kaz took refuge at one of the safe houses in Carol City and began coordinating his trip out of town. He heard noises emanating in the garage of the house. He thought he was alone and was taken by surprise.

Boobie Boy

He pulled a black Uzi from a nearby closet and proceeded through the kitchen towards the garage. He pointed the Uzi forward and pulled open the garage door. He was shocked to see Beebee sitting on an old beat up sofa with discarded pizza boxes all around him.

"What the fuck you doing here Negro?!" exclaimed Kaz.

"I'm on the run, G," replied Beebee.

"Yeah I saw that shit on the news," said Kaz.

Kaz quickly closed the door and placed the cocked Uzi into the comer. He approached Beebee and could see how nervous he was. He had never seen him in this state and felt bad for him.

"You know your man Charles is a rat? We got busted together and he walked," said Kaz.

"I heard you caught a charge but I didn't know he walked," replied Beebee.

"Yeah man I'm fighting the charges with an entrapment plea," said Kaz. "You think he ratted you out as well?" Inquired Kaz.

"Naw, this is too big, it's national now. I think its Blandon," said Beebee.

"This whole thing we tried to build is crumbling man," said Kaz.

"Yeah and that fucking Hollywood is trying to take advantage of us right now," replied Beebee. "Your nigga Blow is with that nigga, man," he said.

Kaz had not realized that Beebee had maneuvered near the corner and now stood near the cocked Uzi.

"I don't know who to trust now my nigga," he said.

"Whoa, you don't think I had anything to do with that," said Kaz.

"I got to tie up loose in ends," said Beebee.

Kaz could see that Beebee was now babbling. He seemed to be talking his thoughts out as he spoke.

"Listen, Blow is his own man. I can't control him. You know this business. Look at your boy Blandon," said Kaz.

Beebee seemed to snap out of his befuddlement after the statement. He moved away from the Uzi and flopped down on the sofa.

"I guess you're right," he replied.

Boobie Boy

"Listen, let me talk to my lawyer and see what's going on out there," said Kaz. "I'm facing charges just like you."

Kaz left the garage and phoned his lawyer. The lawyer said Blandon was working with the CIA before his DEA arrest. Kaz reasoned he had been setting up Beebee the entire time by supplying him with cheap drugs for distribution. Blandon used the funds from the drug game to fund a war in his own home country. Beebee was just a fall guy, a Patsy in case he got in trouble while in the U.S. transacting business.

Kaz realized that they all were just pawns playing at the expense of larger entities. He was destroying his neighborhood and his people to fund a war. In his ignorance he chased the American dream to the detriment of his people. He felt a certain betrayal by those in authority and was enraged by it.

He slammed the phone to the receiver. He and many others had lost years on their lives to the prison system. Drugs and crime ravished the community due to the greed of young jobless men. They placed their dreams and aspirations into an illegal product which was made readily available to them by the government.

Kaz heard what sounded like a loud bomb go off in the room. He smelled smoke and felt a blinding pain go through his head. He could taste blood as it trickled down the back of his throat. He could feel himself began to gag as if he was about to choke. He fell to his knees on the floor of the safe house. He saw what looked like a pitch-black cloak flutter over his eyes and then total darkness.

Thank you for reading Boobie Boy and be sure to leave a review. Also check out other titles from Thomas Barr Jr. and more at www.Printhousebooks.com

Thomas Barr, Jr.

Get the 1st three releases from the *Miami's Urban Chronicles* series; Volume I by *Thomas Barr Jr.*

PrintHouseBooks.com
Read it! Enjoy it! Tell A Friend!
Atlanta, GA.

www.ingramcontent.com/pod-product-compliance
Lightning Source LLC
Chambersburg PA
CBHW022115090426
42743CB00008B/854